UNDER THE SHADE OF THE TREES

UNDER THE SHADE OF THE TREES:

Thomas (Stonewall) Jackson's
Life at Jackson's Mill

By Dennis Norman

Mountain State Press
Charleston, West Virginia

International Standard Book Number: 0-941092-40-2

Library of Congress Catalog Card number: 99-075828

First Edition

Cover by Sharon Harms

Pen & ink drawings by Darryl D. Dean

Photos by Dennis Norman

Mountain State Press
c/o The University of Charleston
2300 MacCorkle Avenue, S.E.
Charleston, WV 25304

Printed in the United States of America

This is a Mountain State Press book produced in affiliation with the University of Charleston, Charleston, West Virginia. Mountain State Press is solely responsible for editorial decisions.

Dedicated to

**My wife Jeanne and my son Mark
for their encouragement and support**

Table of Contents

FORWORD

John Esten Cooke, in his biography of Stonewall Jackson said, "The events of Jackson's life up to the commencement of the late war are not sufficiently interesting to justify very extended notice." Fortunately, most of Jackson's biographers did not agree with him. However, with few exceptions, they ignored his formative years.

The story of young Tom Jackson is most certainly worth telling for here we find the events that would mold the man who became the great tactician of the Confederate Army. Only one author has made any significant effort to accurately record those early days: Dr. Roy Bird Cook. He was a pharmacist and newspaper editor who wrote *The Family and Early Life of Stonewall Jackson in 1924.* Dr. Cook's notes and collection of documents and letters were a primary source for this volume.

I have ignored the genealogy of the Jackson family, in deference to Dr. Cook's definitive work on the subject. Instead I have concentrated on a chronological record of the events that were experienced by young Tom Jackson during his life at Jackson's Mill. While the incidents recorded in this book are well documented, some literary license has been taken in an effort to bring warmth to cold, hard fact. Therefore certain chapters contain an attempt to expose the thoughts of this young orphan who feared he might never make anything of himself.

While every effort has been made to remove the sugar coating that has been applied by the majority of Jackson biographers, especially the very early ones, some of it still remains. Those stories so encrusted, which escape all verification, have not been included. The fact remains, however, that just as General Stonewall Jackson was an exceptional man, young Tom Jackson was an exceptional boy.

The title of this book is, of course, taken from the last words spoken by Jackson as he lay dying in the chandler's office at Guiney Station, Virginia. Many believe he was talking about the West Fork River and his beloved grove of maples at Jackson's Mill when he said, "Let us cross over the river, and rest under the shade of the trees." I believe it as well.

D.L. Norman

Jackson's Mill, West Virginia

September 1999

"3D"

CHAPTER ONE

Mother

The woman in the bed was covered with heavy quilts to ward off the cold December drafts that found their way into the small room. The dark brown hair that fell away on the pillow was streaked with white and the once bright gray eyes were rheumy. She looked ten years older than the thirty-three years that she was.

The children standing at the foot of the bed were not even sure that she could see them, but then she raised a thin hand and motioned them to her. Warren, the eldest at ten years, moved to one side of the sickbed while his brother and sister, seven-year-old Tom and five-year-old Laura Ann, crowded against the other.

Julia Beckwith Neale, wife to Jonathan Jackson for nine years and now wife to Blake B. Woodson since November 4, 1830, was dying. The son she had given to Woodson in the fall had sapped her strength and further damaged her already frail health.[1] Her face was colorless and each breath was taken in quick, shallow gasps. The Neale family had always feared for their daughter's health. She had been prone to pulmonary trouble and the shock of losing both her first husband and oldest child, Elizabeth, to typhoid fever, within twenty-one days had caused a deep bereavement with a lasting physical impact. The recent years of loneliness, marriage to a much older man and separation from her children had been too much to bear.

When she married Blake Woodson, an attorney and county clerk of Fayette County, he had convinced her that his low salary and small one-story house would not support them all, so her sons had been sent to stay with relatives. Tom pressed close against the bed and took his mother's hand. Memories of his parting from her the year before came back like crystal and he could see her crying bitterly as he rode away on a horse behind one of his uncle's slaves.

Now it was his face wet with tears and this time it would be his mother who would leave him. Tom looked at Warren. He was handling this well, so much like a man. Laura seemed confused and did not appear to understand what was happening.

In short, labored breaths their mother told them how much she had missed them, how much she would always love them. She spoke of their father and sister Elizabeth as if they were standing there. She asked the children for a promise; that each of them would love, obey and consecrate their lives to God. The children readily agreed and held their mother while she said a special prayer for them, one that Thomas Jackson would remember for the rest of his life.

Later that evening, on Saturday, December 2, 1831, sometime between eight and nine at night, Julia Beckwith Neale gave in to the struggle and died quietly. The next day, Sunday, she was buried in West Lake cemetery near Ansted. It would be twenty-four years before Tom Jackson would stand near his mother's grave again.

He visited the graveyard in the summer of 1855. It was one of the great sorrows of his life that he could not remember, nor could anyone tell him, exactly which grave was that of his mother. The fact of whether or not he eventually found the location has been argued by several of his biographers but Jackson settles the dispute himself in a letter to his sister on March 31, 1856. *"I wish to put stones on his [Warren Jackson's] grave and also father's and sister's and also on mother's if I knew certainly the spot."*

Julia Jackson's grave remained unmarked until after the Civil War when one of the faithful members of Jackson's Stonewall Brigade erected a monument at his own expense.

Unfortunately, the placement was guesswork and the date of

her death carved on the stone is incorrect.

CHAPTER TWO

Cummins Jackson

Blake B. Woodson did not long survive his wife and the children were left to the care of their stepfather's half brother William C. Woodson. It seems neither the Neales, Jacksons, nor the Woodsons had been happy about the marriage in the first place and it was not long before William Woodson wrote to the Neale family asking them to come for the children. In the meantime, Woodson eased them out of his life by sending them to stay with a family by the name of Buster. In his letter to Thomas Neale of Parkersburg, Julia's father, was very brusque. He wrote, "*Come after the children or they will be bound out!*"

After checking with the Jackson side of the family, Thomas Neale made arrangements with two business friends, who were traveling that way, to stop at the Buster home and bring the children to Parkersburg. When the two men arrived, they were informed that the Jackson children were no longer there. A Mr. Cummins Jackson[2] of Jackson's Mill in Lewis County had collected them some ten days before. This news, when it reached him several days later, was not well received by the children's grandfather.

Neale was soon in contact with an attorney, Lewis Maxwell, who maintained a law office in Weston, Virginia, some five miles south of Jackson's Mill. His letter to Maxwell was not at all flattering to Cummins Jackson. Referring to his daughter's view of Cummins, Neale wrote, *"He would be the last man in the world, if she was living, to have her children—for she spoke of him in the most contemptible terms."* Alluding to past troubles over the children between Julia Jackson and Cummins Jackson, the agitated grandfather of Tom Jackson wrote that the lawyer should *"see if he will give them up. If not I want you to take such steps against him as will compel him."*

Neale also expressed concern about what "breeding and manners" they might acquire at the hands of Cummins and was at a total loss to understand why the man would want the children at all. *"Unless,"* he wrote to the attorney, *"He wants to make drudges of them."*

In the meantime Warren had returned to his Uncle Alfred Neale in Parkersburg while Tom and Laura were happily installed with their grandmother Jackson, two maiden aunts and several uncles at Jackson's Mill. At their disposal were over 4,000 acres of land, saw and grist mills, a large two-story log house, a blacksmith shop, horses, cattle and nine slaves. All of this was owned by the man held in such great contempt by the Neales, Cummins E. Jackson.

An old saw mill similar to the one owned by Cummins

Jackson is presently housed on the lower floor of the

gristmill.

Cummins Jackson was Jonathan Jackson's half brother, born in 1802, twelve years after the birth of Tom Jackson's father. He was over six feet by two or three inches and possessed a stout but athletic body. He was opinionated, industrious and, as one acquaintance stated in print, "…utterly devoid of Christianity."

Without any doubt this last disposition was a major point of contention in the rocky relationship with his sister-in-law. He had most of the vices of men who lived the supposedly carefree bachelor life in the mid-nineteenth century but pursued none of them to excess. All agreed that this big man with the beardless face and striking blue-gray eyes was a firm friend and a bitter enemy. While holding no political aspirations for himself, he controlled many of those who did through the influence that accrues to a wealthy man.

Additionally, he was no stranger to litigation and would passionately pursue his objectives in the courts. Though a liberal and giving man, Cummins Jackson did not race his horses for sport nor enter a game of chance for the fun of it. He was genuinely fond of money. This fondness for money would later cause his death. Along with a large group of men, from Lewis County, Cummins Jackson joined the gold rush in 1849 and died of a fever contracted in a gold camp at Shasta, California on December 4, 1849.

Cummins Jackson may have been looking forward to the legal battle with Thomas Neal over custody of the children but other problems began to occupy the Neal family and the effort to "compel him to give them up" was never undertaken. In the meantime, Thomas and Laura were under the care of the uncle: politico, land baron, sportsman and entrepreneur.

CHAPTER THREE

Homestead

The West Fork of the Monongahela River turns sharply to the north at Weston and meanders in that general direction for some four or five miles before it swings to the west for 1500 feet and then abruptly loops back to the north creating a horseshoe bend.[3]

In the landmass that filled this horseshoe Edward Jackson, Cummins's father, had built a large two-story log house. Here on the north side of the river there was a significant tract of nearly level land suitable for gardens and orchards. On the south side of the river was a great meadow with groves of sugar maples and locust trees and large sycamores that stood like sentinels at numerous points along the riverbank.

In 1808, Cummins's father, Edward Jackson, built an eight-foot high dam across the West Fork in the lower arc of the horseshoe bend. On the east side of the river, against the base of the steep hills, he constructed a gristmill. Later, he decided to move the mill to the west bank and there he constructed a forty-by-forty foot frame building that housed two flour mills, two bolting machines and two horizontal mill wheels. Thirty feet or so to the south of the grist mill, opposite the dam, Jackson built a saw mill and furnished the lumber for most of the houses and stores in the community.

On Christmas day, 1828, Edward Jackson, millwright, farmer, surveyor, Colonel of Militia, sheriff and Virginia assemblyman, died intestate. With no will and money owed, Jackson's mills were sold to pay off debts and Cummins Jackson, who should have inherited the property, had to buy it. The force of the water coursing through the sharp bend of the river soon undermined the mill's foundation and it slipped into the river. The dam fared no better and Cummins Jackson had to replace it in 1833.

In the years that followed, Cummins added more and more tracts of land to his already significant holdings in this green, lush spot in the West Fork River valley. As his holdings increased so did his influence in the community.

The house that Tom and Laura Jackson came home to was a twenty-by-forty foot, two-story log affair with huge fireplaces at either end. The structure was set on a rise well back from the unpredictable river that Indians had named the "Muddy Water." The road from Weston ran near the house and curved north at the gristmill where it began a gradual descent to the ford some 450 feet below the dam. Years later Cummins Jackson would build a much larger home some three hundred feet closer to the mill where the road began its curve toward the ford.

Jackson's Mill on the West Fork River in Lewis County,

West Virginia.

At the homestead Tom and Laura met again with their Jackson relatives: Grandmother Elizabeth Drake Jackson, Uncle James Madison Jackson, Uncle Edward J. Jackson, Uncle Andrew Jackson and Aunt Peggy Jackson who was soon to be married. Old Robinson, the slave who had taken Tom away from his home in Clarksburg after his mother's marriage to Woodson, was there along with his wife, "Granny" Nancy Robinson. There were seven other slaves who worked either in the mills or in the big house.

The small community had its own store and several miles down river was the Broad Run Baptist Church that offered numerous social events along with weekly doses of fire and brimstone preaching. School was wherever room could be found and whenever someone could be found to teach.

The area abounded with interesting characters. There were revolutionary war veterans still living and men of the times with names well known in the halls of power. An easy walk to the north would bring you to the little community of Westfield where the writer, Alexander Scott Withers, made his home. Withers, who looked like the scholar he was, with nose and chin curving toward each other and an unruly mop of hair, would have a significant impact on the life of Tom Jackson.

It was a gentle, pastoral scene and it is hard to imagine that the life of the two young orphans in a house full of adults could have been anything but utopian.

CHAPTER FOUR

Under the Shade of the Trees

Just across the river, in the big south meadow, was a grove of large sugar maples. Trees, at least for young boys, are meant to be climbed and sugar maples are designed by mother nature for that purpose. In addition to that particular recreation, the maples offered cool shade in summer. In late winter and early spring they produced a thin sap that tasted wonderful when boiled down in large copper kettles. Young Tom immediately adopted the grove as his own private place and spent many hours in its shadows during the summer. In the early spring when the sap began to run he would carve spigots from sumac limbs and drive them into holes he had bored in his beloved trees, gathering sap for the kettles that sat over raging fires.

There was no bridge spanning the river at the mill and access to the south meadow was gained only by boat or by fording. One day Tom decided that he should have his own craft and with the help of old Robinson he built a small dugout canoe. He had selected a large log that had been rejected at the sawmill and with fire and ax hollowed out the trunk in the form of a small boat.

Many times he paddled Laura and himself across the river to the south meadow. The spring following their arrival turned out to be very wet and after one great thunderstorm Tom set out for the south meadow in his dugout, fighting a frightful current. Halfway across the raging river Tom lost control of his boat and was quickly swept over the dam. Fortunately the water was not very deep there and Tom alternately swam and walked to the shore.

Laura, too, delighted in these outdoor adventures and often would help Tom catch live rabbits by chasing them up a hollow log and stopping up both ends. Fishing was not only a major pastime but offered Tom a way to earn money. The West Fork teemed with bass, blue gill, pike and catfish. Tom was, by all accounts, an excellent fisherman. He had an agreement with a man named Kester, the gunsmith in Weston, to sell him any extra fish he might catch for fifty cents each provided the fish was at least twelve inches long.

One day Tom landed a twenty-four inch pike and decided to take it in to Kester. Along the way he was stopped by a man who admired the fish and offered to give him a dollar for it. Tom refused the offer and explained that the fish was already sold. Not to be denied, the gentleman then offered Tom two dollars for the pike saying that was most certainly more than he could hope to get for it in Weston.

It was very tempting but Tom again refused the offer and told the man that many times the Weston gunsmith had paid him fifty cents for fish that weren't quite twelve inches and this one would go a long way to make up the difference. Even Kester was impressed with the large pike and offered Tom a dollar for it.

"Nope," said Tom, "We have already struck a bargain for fifty cents and a deal is a deal."

Life at Jackson's Mill was wonderful for young Tom Jackson. There were, he said years later, "None to give their mandates; none for me to obey but as I chose; surrounded by my playmates and relatives, all apparently eager to promote my happiness."[4]

He was free to do as he wished, to daydream in the shade of his maple trees, to watch the millers at work, to play with his collie dog or carve cornstalk fiddles. Not that there wasn't work for the young boy to do, chores on a farm can be endless and Tom did his share, but no one ever forced work upon him.

One evening in the early summer of 1833, Tom and Laura mounted his horse Lucy for a short ride to a neighbor's party. Along the way they had to pass an old deserted shack that was said to be haunted. As they neared the spot, the horse balked at an object in the road, something that began to grow in height even as they watched.

"Who's there?" Tom yelled.

But the white apparition did not answer, it simple continued to get even taller.

"Who's there?" Tom demanded again.

By now the white specter in front of him had grown to a great height and was developing wings. Quickly, Tom turned his horse, which needed little encouragement and clattered back up the road toward home. Later that evening Tom and Laura learned, amid much laughter, that their Uncle

Edward, who was fond of practical jokes, had played the part of the frightful specter.

In August of 1833 an event occurred that abruptly halted Tom's idyllic life at Jackson's Mills. Grandmother Elizabeth Brake Jackson, who had loved and mothered the children, died at the age of sixty-three. Laura spent some time with her local aunts but was soon taken to live with her Uncle Alfred Neale, in Parkersburg. Not long after, Tom was sent to Harrison County to live with his Uncle Isaac and Aunt Polly Brake.[5] Tom was eleven years old and heartbroken. It was happening all over again.

CHAPTER FIVE

Adventure

Thomas Jackson's welcome to the Isaac Brake home was rather cool. Brake, reportedly a stern disciplinarian, may have "laid down the law" in short order and overwhelmed the young boy who had, for some years, "none to obey but as I chose." At any rate Tom soon slipped away and returned to the mill for a short visit. Uncles, slaves and all were glad to see him and it must have been difficult for him to return to his Uncle Brake's farm a few days later. Soon thereafter an incident occurred that caused the boy to leave his uncle for good. Tom Jackson would never speak of it to anyone. Speculation was that the event involved some breach of

Tom's religious principles, an undeserved whipping or a disagreement over chores.

Thomas Jackson's nephew and namesake, Thomas Jackson Arnold, suspected his uncle left Isaac Brake because he had been forced to ride a wild mule one Sunday. He received the fright of his young life when the animal first threw him to the ground and then jumped over him. But these are only speculations and no one will ever know for sure.

Whatever the reason it was sufficient enough for Tom to pack his meager belongings and go to the home of his father's cousin in Clarksburg. There he asked for, and received, his dinner. Judge John Jackson and his wife pressed for details of the problem with no success. All the boy would say was, "Uncle Brake and I can't agree. I have quit him and shall not go back again."

After dinner he took his leave and went to spend the night with his favorite cousin before setting out once again for the people and the place he loved most of all, Jackson's Mill.

Once back at what he always called his "adopted home," Tom Jackson took up where he had left off. For his twelfth birthday on January 21, 1836 he was given a small flock of sheep and of course was busy making plans and carving spouts for the coming sap season. Cummins Jackson, now knowing for certain that Tom was his to raise, hired a school teacher to teach at the mill and it was here that the small spark of desire for knowledge was fanned into a bright flame for the young orphan by a man called Robert Ray. He taught Tom and several other local children in one of the little outbuildings near the grist mill. For the first time young Tom Jackson was exposed to formal education.

That fall his brother Warren, who at the age of sixteen was teaching school in Buckhannon, stopped by Jackson's Mill. He was on his way to Parkersburg to see Laura and wished to know if Tom would like to come along.

From the homestead in Weston the trip would cover almost one hundred miles. Cummins Jackson, who thought Warren mature and steady and who couldn't say no to an eager Tom Jackson, gave them food and money, mounted Tom on one of his best horses and sent the boys off with his blessing. After an uneventful and leisurely trip the Jackson brothers arrived at Parkersburg on the eastern bank of the Ohio River. Tom's Uncle, Alfred Neale, lived on James Island, a short distance away, on a tract of over one hundred and fifty acres that he and a brother cleared and farmed together.

The farm was almost entirely paid for, according to Uncle Alfred, by selling cleared timber as cordwood to the many steamboats that traveled the river. The Jackson boys listened to Alfred Neale's stories with interest and soon hatched a plan to make their fortune. They would travel down river, find their own deserted island and cut and sell firewood to the steamboats just as their uncles had. It would be a great adventure!

The boys finished their visit in high excitement and went down river to the town of Belleville, where they stayed with their Uncle George and Aunt Rebecca White, who was Jonathan Jackson's youngest sister, for a few weeks while they refined their plans.

Once on their way they visited and rejected a number of islands until they discovered one on the Mississippi River just off the southwest corner of Kentucky, that seemed to suit their needs. They set up housekeeping in a deserted log cabin and soon had contracts to cut cordwood for passing steamboats.

For the rest of fall and part of that winter Tom and Warren Jackson chopped and sold wood. They were young and alone and the work was hard. Each boy passed a birthday there in January of 1837. Tom became thirteen and Warren seventeen. It was not at all pleasant on their swampy little island and before long both boys became sick. By February they decided that they had had enough and caught a steamer bound for Parkersburg where they again stopped at the home of their uncle on James Island.

Just how much of a fortune was made by the two brothers will never be known, for neither would say much about their adventures. They had made some money, however, and each boy purchased a new trunk, but it is doubtful there was much to put in either one of them. Tom gave his trunk to his sister Laura before he returned to Jackson's Mill. Warren gave his to their half-brother Wirt Woodson.

Tom and Warren stayed at the Neales' for some time, regaining the weight they had lost and overcoming their fevers. Tom seemed to recover quickly but Warren was slow to mend and eventually decided to return to Upshur County, where he stayed with his Aunt Rachel and Uncle Jacob Brake and resumed teaching.

Tom's stay on the desolate island and the long hours of hard work had given him time to think. He was ready to return to Jackson's Mill to those who loved and were loved by him, and to pursue the education that he now knew he must have. The real adventure was about to begin, and it would be found in books at the hands of men like Robert Ray and not on some mosquito-infested island, a place he decided, he never wanted to see again. Years later in September of 1846, when he was a new Second Lieutenant of Company K, First U.S. Artillery Regiment, he would see the island from the deck of a steamboat, taking him on his way to fight in the Mexican War.

CHAPTER SIX

Getting an Education

After he returned to Jackson's Mill, Tom spent his days sitting at the end of the dam or near the millrace, sometimes reading and sometimes not. He prowled through his beloved grove of maple trees and occasionally helped around the farm and in the sawmill or gristmill. Mostly he spent those solitary days in deep thought and was not moved from this arcane introspection until mid-summer when he was offered a job.

The Parkersburg-Stauton Turnpike was under construction in Lewis County and Minter Bailey, a commissioner of construction, hired Tom to assist with surveying. Bailey, who owned a hotel in Weston, worked Tom long hours but compensated by teaching him a smattering of engineering and the use of survey equipment. Jackson labored through the summer and earned a reputation as a young man who worked hard and did exactly what he was told to do.

That fall a school was established in Westfield, less than a mile from the Cummins Jackson farm. Tom immediately enrolled and received two months of the three R's under the guidance of a Mr. Mills. It was during this short term that Tom had his first taste of physical combat. One morning on the way to school another local boy accosted two young girls, and was generally making a nuisance of himself. Tom, who had been walking with the girls, warned the bigger boy off. When that warning was ignored, young Jackson sprang upon the bully and struck him enough times to send him off howling.

When the short term was over Tom was described as

one who was slow to learn but had a remarkably high retention rate. He was also, noted the teacher, very determined.

By December a schoolmaster named Phillip Cox, Jr., took on some half-dozen pupils in Westfield. He taught writing, geography, arithmetic, reading and spelling. Master Cox soon discovered that not only did this young Jackson orphan like arithmetic, he was especially good at it.

By the spring of 1839 Tom was back in his Maple Grove harvesting sap for maple sugar. He helped around the mills and rode a horse to Weston each week to fetch the mail and borrow books. These he devoured under the shade of his trees or propped up against a sycamore that towered on the bank at the end of the dam. He also rode his uncle's horses in the many races that were held in the county. One of the tracks he liked best was on the Cummins Jackson farm.

That summer Tom was scheduled to ride one of his uncle's thoroughbreds in what was touted as the race of the year. The Jackson horse, named Kit, would be up against an equally popular mount from the Simmons farm on Freeman's Creek. Both horses were known to be fast and betting was higher than normal. Cummins Jackson did not like to lose at anything and in particular he didn't like losing a horse race. So it was probably at his instigation that two of his slaves went to the Simmons farm and "borrowed" Kit's opponent long enough to run a practice race, which Kit won.

Tom, set to ride Kit in the big race, was mortified when he discovered what his uncle was up to and immediately refused to jockey the mount. An argument ensued and Cummins Jackson declared he would ride Kit himself. But Cummins was a big man and the extra weight slowed the famous Kit enough to allow the victory to go to the other horse. Needless to say there were many unhappy people at the track that day. However, the argument did nothing to injure the relationship between nephew and uncle.

Tom Jackson admired and loved his Uncle Cummins and, in fact, considered him a surrogate father.

That fall another two-month term of school was announced. It would be held in the Lewis County courthouse by Colonel Alexander Scott Withers, a resident of Westfield, who was a frequent visitor to Cummins Jackson home. Withers, author of *"Chronicles of Border Warfare,"* was a consummate storyteller and a genuine scholar who never missed an opportunity to talk of his Alma mater, William and Mary College.

Tom didn't miss a day of class and so impressed Withers that the scholar loaned him many of his precious books. Tom's favorite book, however, continued to be the Bible and, as he would admit later in a letter to his Aunt Clementine Neale, the idea of becoming a minister was being seriously considered.

In the meantime, between sessions of school, Tom worked on the farm and in the mills. His social life included barn-raisings, corn-huskings, apple-peelings, and hunting with his uncles for deer and bear. Tom enjoyed corn-huskings where men and women of the community gathered in a neighbor's barn to pull the husk from ears of corn. The shucked corn was piled on the floor and when a man found a red ear of corn he was allowed to kiss the woman of his choice. Later there would be food and drink. Apple peelings occurred in the fall when apples were peeled and quartered in order to make apple butter. Several groups of neighbors sat around washtubs, they would fill with apples, exchanging gossip and telling stories while they worked.

On January 21, 1840 he celebrated his sixteenth birthday. His brother Warren was unable to attend the festivities as he was under a doctor's care in Buckhannon. The doctor thought Warren had consumption, another name for tuberculosis.

CHAPTER SEVEN

Down-river Friend

The West Fork River dropped rapidly after passing over the six-foot-high dam at Jackson's gristmill. The river's increased velocity and unimpaired volume suggested that additional mills could be built along its banks and, in the spring of 1840, another mill was constructed several miles downstream near the mouth of Broad Run.6 The man who built the new gristmill was Benjamin Lightburn. He had moved into Lewis County, Virginia, from Pennsylvania. Among his children was sixteen-year old Joseph Andrew Jackson Lightburn, born on September 21, 1924.

Not long after meeting his new neighbor, Tom

Jackson found that they had several things in common. Both worked in a mill, each had a passion for reading and more than a passing interest in religion. Of less interest but surely a topic of conversation, they were both were born on the twenty first day of the month in the same year; Tom in January and Joe in September.

It was through this friendship that, aside from the stories told and retold by the county's revolutionary war veterans, Tom was first exposed to military history. Joe Lightburn owned a copy of *"The Life of Francis Marion- The Swamp Fox of Revolutionary War Fame"* by Mason Weems, which he considered one of his most precious possessions. It was this volume that completely engrossed Jackson, as he and Joe Lightburn sat on the riverbank at the end of the dam, reading together. They were oblivious to the roar of the water and the steady thump of the mill wheels.

They were soon fast friends and they gathered the other local youngsters and played at war and participated in deer and bear hunts with the men. And, of course, as good friends do, they traded their innermost secrets. Tom revealed his nearly physical pain at the loss of his mother and affirmed that he would never, in his entire life, forget her deathbed admonition that he should always be true to God.

With some sadness he told his new friend that he believed his Uncle Cummins thought him to be somewhat dull-witted and therefore paid less attention to his education than that of his sister and brother. Not that his uncle hadn't been good to him. He had, and for that Tom would love his uncle and stand by him always, even if he didn't go to church. Tom's future must lie in the ministry, he confided to Joe, perhaps as some sort of soldier for the Lord. How great it would be, Tom thought, to die in battle while engaged in a great religious crusade.

Joe confessed that he, too, was interested in the Lord's work but that his desire was to become a famous military leader like Francis Marion, the Swamp Fox. To that end, he declared, he would someday attend the military academy at West Point.

Together Tom and Joe regularly attended meetings at the Broad Run Baptist Church and had numerous discussions about religion. Some of them may have been heated since Tom openly professed a preference for the Presbyterian doctrine over that of the Baptist.

Material on their friendship is sparse and very little exists that can document the strength of it beyond 1841. During a trip to Parkersburg in August of 1841, Tom was approached by a man called Uncle Watty Smith who asked about Joe Lightburn's father. He was curious about Benjamin Lightburn and in particular wanted to know what political party he belonged to. Tom replied that he didn't know but that he supposed him to be an Old Hickory Democrat since he had named one son Joseph Andrew Jackson. This reticence is curious, to say the least, and one must wonder if the friendship may have been dissolving. If indeed the discussions on religion had caused some fracture between the two boys then it may have been further exacerbated when they competed against each other for the single opening to the military academy at West Point early the following year. Whatever the true course of their friendship, the two went their own ways. (For additional information on Joe Lightburn see Appendix A)

CHAPTER EIGHT

"Constable T. Jackson"

Tom Jackson became seventeen on January 21, 1841. He was slim, narrow shouldered and, at five feet, ten inches, considered to be a tall man. His ice-blue eyes did not twinkle as they had several years ago and there was a seriousness about him that belied his years. His priorities were different now; education, religion and money held particular interest for the boy who was thinking of becoming a minister. All the dreams of his youth did not fade in adulthood. In 1852, when he was twenty-eight, wrote to his Aunt Clementine Neale that, "I should not be surprised were I to die upon a foreign field clad in ministerial armor, fighting under the banner of Jesus."

Work on the farm and in the mill kept him busy but did not do much for his financial situation. Uncle Cummins provided food, clothing, shelter and educational expenses and was generous to a fault when money was required for some reason. But Tom did not expect, nor did he receive, much recompense for his work around the homeplace.

The summer before, Alexander Scott Withers, the Jackson's writer friend and neighbor, had been appointed Justice of the peace in Lewis County. In the spring of 1841, the new Justice suggested to Cummins Jackson that Tom would be a good candidate for the appointed office of Constable in Freeman's Creek district. Tom was interested in the position and early that summer members of the county court met to decide on the appointments. The Jacksons were astounded when the court, by an overwhelming vote, gave the appointment to a neighbor. But Cummins Jackson was not fond of defeat and very quickly brought his financial and political power to bear on the members of the court who had not voted for his nephew. No records exist but the best speculation indicates that a number of those who voted against Tom were forced to reconsider because they owed money or favors to Cummins Jackson. Within five days the court had changed its decision and Thomas Jackson was duly appointed Constable for Lewis County.

As constable, Tom served warrants, collected debts and fines in the Freeman's Creek district and recorded who had paid and how much. It was not a glamorous job by any means but it gave him an independent income and he was kept busy that summer. His duties allowed him sufficient free time to visit his ailing brother in Buckhannon and to do a small amount of work for his uncle.

The position also offered the opportunity to spend a good deal of time in Weston where he was often seen in deep discussion with one or more of the city's notable residents.

Tom, like his family, was a staunch Democrat and a number of those talks became heated, probably because, as his cousin, Sylvanus White would later write, "Thomas could not stand to have his word disputed."

For the most part his tenure as constable was mundane. The only incident of any note that occurred involved a widow who had sold several items to a man who was not really in a position to pay for them. He was, in fact, a chronic debtor and the sum he owed the widow was merely a drop in the bucket compared to the total he owed around the county.

The widow swore out a warrant and Tom served it on the man who told Jackson that he would pay the debt shortly. Several more visits to the man's farm brought the same response and each time the young constable left empty-handed.

One day, several weeks later, Tom happened to be in Weston when he saw the debtor coming down the street on horseback. Tom watched as the man rode up at the livery stable and dismounted. He was in the act of tying the reins to a hitching post when he looked up and saw the constable approaching. Knowing that the lawman was intent on seizing his horse to cover the debt, he quickly stepped back from the hitching rail and vaulted into the saddle.

As the man pulled the horse away, Tom jumped, caught the bridle, and asked the rider to dismount. The man ordered Tom to release his grip and immediately began to swing at him with a leather riding whip. Tom threw up an arm to ward off the blows and quickly led the horse into the stable where the low overhang of the double doors knocked the man from the saddle. Aware that not only could he lose his horse but that he might even go to jail for his assault on the constable, the man produced the money he owed and offered an apology. Tom accepted both and sent the man on his way.

At about thirty cents for each warrant he served, Tom was

certainly not getting rich but he was making some money,

meeting lots of people and learning to deal with the problems

of the adult world.

CHAPTER NINE

The Raven

Sometime during midsummer of 1841 a small piece of the machinery that moved the great millstones broke. Even though the workmen were able to jury-rig a replacement, Cummins Jackson ordered a new part from Pittsburgh and asked that it be sent by steamship to Parkersburg. The part was due to arrive on August third.

When his uncle asked, Tom quickly agreed to make the nearly one-hundred-mile journey and bring back the new part for the mill. It would give him a break from his duties as constable and it would allow him to see his sister.

On Sunday, August the first, Tom rose early and rode

to his Aunt Katy Williams' home in Clarksburg. He brought an extra horse with him in the hope that his friend Thaddeus Moore would make the trip with him. After meeting with Moore and laying plans the two boys attended services at the Presbyterian Church and then prepared for an early start the next day. According to a journal that Moore kept of the trip, Thad met Tom at his Aunt Katy's home where a broken cinch strap on Moore's saddle caused some delay. Further delay resulted when Moore had to pick up his saddlebags at the shop where he had left them to be repaired.

Irritated at the lost time, Tom set a quick pace out of Clarksburg and did not slow until they reached Randolph's Tannery in Salem. After a brief rest the boys rode down the pike, Tom impatiently tapping his horse with the riding whip at every step. Several hours later the two young men stopped at Neeley's Inn for dinner and again Tom had to urge Thad on, repeating that he must be on the banks of the Ohio River by the next afternoon. Moore was probably loath to leave because of Neeley's daughter Mary. Who he describes, in his journal, as a "handsome, modest and intelligent young lady with the most beautiful black sparkling eyes."

That evening, just before dark, they rode into Pennsboro and stopped for the night at Martin's Inn, a large two-story stone house that featured good food and pleasant accommodations. Inside, the lamps had just been lighted and a few guests were already eating their supper. One of those guests was a very tall man with a massive head of graying hair and stern features. He was quickly introduced to the two boys by a bubbling Mrs. Martin who was obviously thrilled at having such a great personage staying in her establishment. It was, said the innkeeper, Sam Houston of Texas.

Houston asked the boys to join him when he heard the Jackson name and proceeded to quiz Tom about his relatives. The hero of the battle of San Jacinto and former President of Texas asked about Joseph Jackson, an old congressional colleague. Tom told him that a family friend,

Samuel Hayes, had taken Joseph Jackson's seat in the House of Representatives.

The boys spent the rest of the evening listening to the former president talk of his days with the Cherokee Indians and how he had been adopted by the tribe and given the name of "The Raven." Houston spent a good deal of time talking about Texas politics and hotly denounced the policies of current Texas President Mirabeau Lamar. He admitted that he was again a candidate for that office and had every reason to believe that he would once again become President of the Republic of Texas. Several months later, the young men were happy to hear that Houston was overwhelmingly elected President by Texas voters.

Throughout the evening Sam Houston told tales of his fantastic life as a lawyer, schoolteacher, congressman, governor, duelist and commander of an army. Finally, stroking his chiseled, clean-shaven face, the great man stood to indicate the mostly one-sided conversation was over.

At six-feet six-inches tall, he towered over the two boys. The forty-eight year old adventurer asked Tom to convey his best wishes to John Jay Jackson, a friend whom he had unsuccessfully attempted to see in Parkersburg that very day. His plans, he told Tom included a business stop in Clarksburg and then on to Rockbridge County and would prevent his return to Texas via Parkersburg. Therefore, he would not have the opportunity to see Jackson. Tom quickly agreed to relay Houston's greeting and reluctantly bid him a good night.

Houston was not about when the boys rose early the next morning, ate a quick breakfast and rode off to the west. Houston was the topic of their discussion for most of the morning as Tom pushed the horses at a brisk walk. They rested the horses at noon and ate a lunch prepared by Mrs. Martin. From a nearby field Thad helped himself to an armful of oats for the horses. Saying that they should not have to be ashamed when they passed the place on the way back, Tom insisted that Thad go to the farmhouse and pay for the oats.

Tom was less talkative that afternoon and said only that he must reach the Ohio before dark and that he was determined to deliver Mr. Houston's message. The boys reached the river in good time where Tom collected the part for the mill machinery and then led Thad to the Neales home, where they were warmly welcomed.

On Wednesday, the fourth of August, Tom and Thad attempted to deliver Sam Houston's message but John Jackson was still away. They walked down to see Tom's Aunt Polly and stopped for some sugar cakes and ginger beer at Glime's Hotel. Later a swim in the Little Kanawha River refreshed the boys before supper.

The next day Tom was able to see John Jackson and deliver Houston's message. Jackson was sorry he had missed the General and quizzed Tom about their evening at Martin's Hotel. The boys finally took their leave and galloped off on the return trip home with Tom again pushing the horses saying that they must reach the stone house by supper time. They made it just before a thunderstorm broke over the Pennsboro area, cooling the August heat and allowing them a good night's sleep.

Again, the next day, Tom pushed the pace and seemed glad to be getting closer to home. He was quite talkative this day and told Thad much about his life at the mill and his family and friends. His Uncle Cummins, Tom related, just could not be persuaded to go to a church meeting but he never objected if Tom went. In fact, he told Thad, he and Joe Lightburn had not missed going to church at Broad Run for more than a year now.

As they neared Clarksburg they stopped along the road at the Adams farm where Mr. Adams was burying one of his slaves, who had died most likely from illness and the lack of medical treatment. The boys talked with the farmer and watched for a while before continuing their journey.

Tom was quiet for some time and then told his friend that he believed that all slaves should be free men with a chance for their own lives. He said Joe Lightburn and he had talked about this and that Joe felt the same way.

Thaddeus Moore was somewhat surprised by his friend's comments and suggested it would be better not to make such views known. After all, he told Tom, if such things were carried out and the slaves freed, "We would have to black our own boots." [7]

CHAPTER TEN

To A Brother

The summer of 1841 ended and Tom's days were filled with the duties of constable and the harvest on the farm. The gristmill was very busy and Cummins Jackson ordered its operation seven days a week, reserving Sunday for families less fortunate than most. These poor farmers could grind their wheat for free.

Cummins Jackson was thinking seriously of building a new house on the farm. The old two-story log house was still sufficient but a larger structure of modern design would give everyone more room and be far more fitting for a man of his position in the county. He told Tom that he planned to build the new house on the same little rise of ground but much closer to the gristmill. Cummins Jackson finally built the new house in 1843. It was a two-story frame house with a wrap-around porch. The house stood until December 3, 1915 when it was destroyed by fire and a granite monument now marks the location.

Tom also taught a term of school late that fall. He was becoming well known for his skill in arithmetic and his adeptness at teaching in particular. During instruction on penmanship he had his students write moralistic phrases like, "A man of words and not of deeds is like a garden full of weeds." Perhaps he was making every effort to emulate his brother Warren who was held in high esteem as a teacher in Upshur County.

Tom was very much worried about his brother. Warren's health had not been good since their abortive adventure on the island and his condition had worsened dramatically in the last year. The doctors, in fact, feared it was consumption. On his last visit to Warren's home on Turkey Run, Tom had been shocked by his brother's gaunt figure and prolonged spells of coughing.

By now religion had become a significant part of Tom Jackson's life. He became fond of quoting short passages from the Bible and continually mentioned the will of providence. His life was changing and he knew it. The future was still undecided and based on the disappointments of the past he was preparing himself for the worst. He still didn't know what he wanted and was painfully aware that his limited education would hold him back no matter what vocation he decided to embrace.

To this confused young man of seventeen, the death of his brother Warren in November of 1841, may have been the catalyst that started Tom Jackson on his road to destiny. At the age of twenty, Warren, the young, well-liked schoolteacher, had succumbed to his consumption, leaving his brother as the head of their shrinking, separated family.

Tom now felt an uncertain weight on his shoulders as he helped make the always-hasty arrangements for burial and penned numerous letters to the relatives. The letter he wrote to his Uncle Alfred Neale and sister Laura was never answered. A further hurt came when he realized that, alone, he did not have enough money to buy his brother a headstone.

As Warren was being laid to rest in the Post Cemetery along the Buckhannon-Clarksburg road, Tom Jackson may have decided that he was not going to meet the same fate. He would trust to providence, oh yes, but he would not sit and wait for it to work. He would grab any opportunity to improve his life. Thomas Jackson *would not* be buried as a penniless schoolteacher.

An abrupt change came over Tom after the death of his brother. He seemed to work even harder than he had before and records show he was extremely busy as a constable. He seldom laughed and more than one person commented on his maturity.

He knew that what he now wanted was success and respect. The success, like that which had been attained by his Uncle Cummins and respect like that of his brother Warren in Upshur County, where friends later named a district for him.

Sometime later Tom Jackson sat down and wrote the words he would have engraved on his brother's tombstone;

WARREN J.

Son of

JONATHAN & JULIA B.

JACKSON

Died

In his twentieth year.

This tablet to a brother is reared by kindred left

—bliss is now above—

by friends on earth bereft.

The remains of the headstone for Warren Jackson are now under the care of the Upshur County Historical Society. This piece was found near the grave and was taken to the Charles Gibson Library for safekeeping. Sometime later it was transferred to the Historical Society. The photo shows less than half the stone purchased by Thomas Jackson for his brother.

CHAPTER ELEVEN

Energy and Intellect

The New Year of 1842 slipped in during a snowstorm, unnoticed by Constable Thomas Jackson as he slept in his upstairs bedroom. On a night table was a receipt for a debt he had collected. It was signed T. Jackson. Since Warren had died Tom had dropped the "Thos." in favor of a simple "T." He was even seriously considering taking his father's name as his middle name. It sounded good when he said it — "Thomas Jonathan Jackson."

His future was still unclear. He didn't mind working on the farm and in the mill, but he wasn't really fond of it either. Besides, like the constable business, there was very little money to be made. The only thing he knew for certain was that he wanted, and needed, a better education. In the meantime he would discharge his duties to his uncle and the county court, fish and hunt with his family and friends and pursue the religious contentment that so far had eluded him. He would continue regular attendance at the Broad Run Church where he enjoyed singing hymns more than listening to the sermon and he would either master or give up the violin which had brought more than a little embarrassment to him during the last several years.

In the spring came momentous news for eighteen-year- old Tom. Congressman Samuel Hayes announced a vacancy in the United States Military Academy at West Point. Not only was this college education free, it offered a monthly salary for those whom attended and a permanent job in the United States Army for all whom graduated. With his usual drive and determination, Tom set out to secure this appointment and he had no reservation about using all the political and financial clout his Uncle Cummins could bring to bear.

Almost immediately Tom found that there were other

young men in Lewis County who were also interested in the position. Several of them had equal or greater political pull and one of them was his friend, Joe Lightburn.

Congressman Hayes, sensing a possible loss of votes through any political rift that might result in the struggle for the appointment, directed Weston resident George Jackson, a veteran of the War of 1812, to proctor an examination for the aspirants. The winner would go to West Point.

Four young men met former army Captain George Jackson in the lobby of the Bailey house in Weston to take the examination. Tom, no doubt, assessed his chances as he looked at the other boys. There was Camden Johnson, who was several years younger than the other three, but had significant political power behind him. Gibson Butcher was a friend and like Tom had a desire for a better education. Also, like Tom, Gibson was an orphan. The third boy was his friend, too. As he watched him talk with the others Tom recalled the many times Joe Lightburn had spoken of his desire to become a military officer.

The results were announced several days later. It was Gibson Butcher who would soon be wearing the gray uniform of a West Point cadet. An outstanding score in mathematics had set him above the other three boys. There is good evidence to believe Tom may have come in second. He was known to be adept at math and that category seemed to be the determining factor in Butcher's selection. It is possible the four young men were nearly equal in all others. That being the case, Tom's math skill must have put him next to Butcher.

Tom was very disappointed but took it in his usual stoic manner. He wished Gibson Butcher success when the new West Point cadet left Lewis County in late May of 1842. Perhaps Tom had not given up all hope for he knew that the appointment was conditional, as Gibson must pass the entry exams before actual admission into the academy.

Gibson Butcher passed the exams, however, and Tom

put the military academy out of his mind. He returned t' his work with fervor, more determined than ever to prepare himself for any future opportunity.

That opportunity wasn't long in coming. One late afternoon in early June a visitor stopped at Jackson's Mill. It was the new cadet Gibson Butcher who told Tom he had resigned from the academy. His sudden exposure to the strict rules and physically demanding life of a West Point cadet had quickly convinced Butcher that it was not for him. He also admitted that the amount of study required was more than he was inclined to do. Therefore, if Tom was still interested, the appointment was again open.

Tom immediately rode into Weston to see Captain George Jackson and several other prominent men of the county. Jonathan M. Bennett, who had loaned numerous books to Tom and advised him on various occasions, listened quietly while Tom told him of Butcher's resignation. When he was finished, Bennett asked Tom if he thought he could handle such a rigid academic life. After all, suggested Bennett, Tom's education to this point was not really sufficient for such an undertaking. Tom told his friend that he knew his education was not the best and that really, by many standards, he was ignorant. However, he was sure that he could make up for it with study. Lots of study.

"I know I have the energy and I think I have the intellect," Tom stated.

Convinced of Tom's sincerity and ability, Bennett and George Jackson decided to make the attempt. They would send young Jackson with every recommendation they could gather. As far as Thomas Jackson was concerned it was already decided - *he was going to West Point.*

CHAPTER TWELVE

The Future Beckons

There was much to do and little time to do it in. Tom felt that Congressman Hayes would support his application for the now vacant position at West Point but he intended to leave nothing to chance. Jackson's mentors quickly produced letters and petitions to Congressman Hayes and Secretary of War Spencer, while Jackson solicited a letter from Gibson Butcher. This was not difficult since the two boys were friends and Butcher felt the need to explain his actions to Congressman Hayes. He also admitted that, in his great haste to leave West Point, he had departed without "reporting myself to the superintendent."

The list of names on the petitions supporting Jackson's admission into the academy were impressive:

Alexander Scott Withers,

Jonathan M. Bennett,

George Jackson,

William J. Bailey,

W.E. Arnold, R.P. Camden,

Minter Bailey,

Matthew Edmiston,

John McWhorter.

All of who were politically and financially important in the area. They were sure to get the attention of the people in Washington. The petitions also, for the first time in print, used a middle initial in Jackson's name, "recommend to his Excellency, the Secretary of War, Thomas J. Jackson as a fit and proper person to receive the appointment of cadet in the military academy at West Point."[8] In an uncharacteristic moment, Tom asked his Uncle Cummins to submit his resignation as constable for him and handed him his records and receipts to turn in to the court. Then, with petitions and letters in hand, Jackson said quick good-byes at the mill, put on his best clothes and rode off to Clarksburg to catch the stage. He had stuffed a pair of saddlebags with essentials and his Uncle Cummins had sent one of his slaves with Tom to bring back the horse. It is also more than likely that the doting uncle gave Tom the money for his ticket on the Pioneer Stage Line.

When Jackson and his companion rode into Clarksburg they found that the only stage for the day had already left. Without hesitation they galloped after it and finally overtook the stage some twelve to fourteen miles later near the city of Grafton. The slave rested the horses and watched Tom clatter off in the coach towards Cumberland, Maryland. East of Cumberland, Tom left the stage and boarded a Baltimore and Ohio train. The train brought him into Washington, D.C., on the seventeenth of June 1842.

The excitement he felt must have been overwhelming. Admission to West Point and a college education, his first train-ride and now he stood in the nation's capital. Asking passers-by for directions, Tom slung his saddlebags over his narrow shoulders and soon found his way to the office of Congressman Samuel Hayes. There he presented his papers.

Hayes had not only been expecting Tom, but had also been working on certain legal requirements necessary for Jackson's admission to West Point. One of the problems was Tom's lack of a legal guardian. Even though his Uncle Cummins Jackson had been taking care of Tom for years, no papers naming him the boy's guardian had ever been filed in the county courthouse. For some reason the Lewis County Court had ignored that history of guardianship and on July 12, 1942, had selected Edward Jackson as Tom's legal guardian. Although he was known to be the boy's favorite uncle, it is not clear why Edward was selected over the much wealthier and politically more powerful Cummins Jackson.

Tom was short on money and accepted a loan from Congressman Hayes while declining an offer to spend several days at the representative's home and see the sights in the nation's capital. Instead Tom made a quick tour of Washington and even climbed up into the unfinished capitol dome. From that vantage point he could and most likely did, see the home of Robert E. Lee in Arlington.

On the eighteenth of June young Jackson traveled to New York City and spent the next day sightseeing. On the twentieth he reported to the military academy at West Point where a clerk added a year to his age and entered him as being

nineteen. He signed the list of new cadets as "Thomas J. Jackson, Weston P.O., Lewis County, Virginia."

Sometime during the next ten days Tom took and passed the entrance exams.[9] He was formally admitted to West Point on July 1, 1842. Among those issued the gray uniforms of a West Point Cadet that summer with Jackson, were Jesse Lee Reno, George B. McClellan, John Gibbons, Ambrose Powell Hill and George Pickett. They would spend four years together learning the art of war and fourteen years later they would practice that art against each other.

Tom Jackson entered his assigned room and immediately removed his homespun coat to counter the July heat that was building in the box-like quarters. He carefully placed his issue of clothing and equipment on the bed nearest the window and tossed his broad-brimmed farmer's hat on top of the pile. His roommate had not reported in yet and for a long time the orphan from Lewis County, Virginia, sat looking out the open window.

Somber thoughts fought to subdue his excitement. He could clearly see the faces of his dead mother and brother. He ached to talk with his sister Laura, to tell her what he had seen and done in just a few short days. He would write soon, he promised himself and when he took leave he would visit.

But those entry exams had been hard and he wondered if he would be able to last long enough to take a leave.

Tom leaned into the breeze blowing through the window with such force that it was snapping the worn curtains. He closed his eyes and imagined himself in his cool grove of maples across the river from the homestead. There, under the shade of the trees, he could rest and think clearly. He could talk with God and work out his problems.

After a few minutes the new cadet opened his eyes and pulled a new notebook from his saddlebags. He sat down at the small desk and wrote "1842" at the top of the page. Then very carefully, he penned a short phrase,

"You may be whatever you resolve to be."

CHAPTER THIRTEEN

A New World

If Tom Jackson had been considered somewhat shy or reticent by his Lewis County neighbors his demeanor at West Point would have to be deemed as that of a classic introvert. He was painfully aware of his awkwardness and lack of formal education. Now, among the erudite young cavaliers like George E. Pickett, Jackson felt so inadequate to the task facing him that he must have been overwhelmed by melancholy. Jackson's homespun clothing marked him as a young man fresh from the farm and the fact that he had paid little attention to his wardrobe since leaving home, made him fair game for a number of upper classmen who hazed him unmercifully. This certainly did nothing for his flagging self-esteem. The class of 1842 was a large one, full of names that, like Jackson's, would be on the lips of the nation within twenty years. McClellan, Reno, Stoneman, Gibbons, Picket, A.P. Hill and Wilcox were, along with Tom Jackson, members of a group of one hundred and nine young men who sought a college education and a commission as a Second Lieutenant in the United States Army that summer.

Two buildings housed the cadets. The north barracks, which was built in 1817, was a stone structure four stories high with forty rooms. Each room was twenty-five by nineteen feet and four cadets were housed in each room. Less than one hundred feet away was the south barracks, also four stories and constructed of stone and stuccoed. It had been built in 1815 and contained fifty rooms, twelve of which were used as offices. Because of their size, thirteen-by-ten feet, the south barracks rooms housed only two cadets each.[10] A sally port ran through the center of the building on the north end, to accommodate the numerous cadets and the second room to the left on the ground floor, was home to Tom Jackson and his roommate, George Stoneman. Stoneman, from the western part of New York was a graduate of the Jamestown Academy and, like his Virginia roommate, was destined for fame. He became a famous Cavalry General for the Union Army, and in 1882, he was elected Governor of California.

An upperclassman neighbor in the south barracks, John Caldwell Tidball, observed Jackson on an almost daily basis for two years and noted Tom Jackson's awkwardness and his excessive blushing. The senior cadet attributed these traits to a very noticeable lack of self-confidence. Considering that Tom was in a new world, peopled mostly by obviously well- educated young men from families farther up the social scale than his own, it is not surprising that Tom kept a self imposed silence and reacted so visibly when he was spoken to.

Additionally, the young Virginian from Jackson's Mill had a frail, high voice and often spoke in a fast and terse manner. It seemed as if he needed to get the conversation over before he might embarrass himself. Those actions, his blushing and manner of speech, along with the fact that Jackson always appeared to go about with his head down in a thoughtful attitude, contributed to the image of someone who suffered a lack of self-confidence. This, however, was the same person who had just recently penned the phrase in his notebook, *"you may be whatever you resolve to be."*

Almost immediately Jackson's will was put to the test. The proper use of English was a mandatory requirement test for Point cadets and an exam on English grammar was scheduled at the end of the first month of the term. Those who failed would be sent home. Jackson passed the test but later told a cousin, "Oh, I tell you, I had to work hard."

As it turned out, Jackson always had to work hard. From the very beginning he applied himself to every task with total energy. At the end of the first year it was obvious as Tom had only fifteen demerits. Out of a class of one-hundred-and-nine that started with Jackson, only seventy-two remained at the end of the first year.

His attention to detail and duty was exemplified by an incident that occurred as the cadets were returning from the battalion mess hall in a small cloudburst. On such occasions the regulations allowed the men to break ranks and dash for cover. Tom Jackson, however, continued to march on alone in solemn cadence getting soaked in the process.

Academically in that first year he ranked forty-fifth in mathematics and seventy in French. In general merit Thomas J. Jackson ranked fifty-one of a class of seventy-two, compared to George Picket and Cadmus Wilcox who ranked fifty-five and fifty-eight respectively.

CHAPTER FOURTEEN

1844 - Home Again

Tom Jackson would spend two years at West Point before he was allowed to come home on leave. Still homesick, however slightly, Tom wrote to his sister Laura in January 1844, "All that I want to render myself happy on earth is the sight of you and my native land. Tell Uncle Cummins if you should see him shortly that I want him to write to me, giving me permission to come home; for without his consent the superintendent will not give me a furlough."

A letter from Tom's Uncle Cummins soon followed and Cadet Jackson was authorized to miss the usual summer encampment to take leave of absence at Jackson's Mill. He

had passed all of his exams, was feeling physically fit and

had a

clearly optimistic view of the future. Tom ranked eighteen in

mathematics, fifty-two in French, sixty-eight in Drawing and

fifty-five in English Grammar. In order of general merit he

had risen from fifty-one to thirty. His roommate, George

Stoneman, was ranked twenty-seven.

Tom wrote to his sister, Laura, "If no change takes

place in the army, and I continue to progress in my class as

well as I have so far, my pay when I leave this institution will

be about one-thousand dollars a year." He was referring to

the fact that those cadets graduating in the upper half of their

class received plum assignments, such as the Dragoons,

where the pay was more. If he had graduated in the lower

half he would have been given an infantry assignment where

the pay was seven hundred and fifty dollars a year instead of

one thousand.

Tom Jackson was in a high fettle — he was a success. He felt good and he was on his way home dressed in a dapper uniform that was sure to impress his family and friends in Lewis County. He was twenty-years-old and full of life.

Jackson was glad to be home again. He was joyfully greeted by everyone at Jackson's Mill and, on trips into Weston, was treated with a respect he had not experienced before.

His happiness at being back among family and friends was so obvious that a cousin suggested he forget about returning to West Point and asked Tom, "Would they send for you if you did not go back?" Tom replied that he thought they would not but he told his cousin, "Not for Lewis County would I fail to go back." He had his hands on an opportunity for a new life and did not intend to give it up willingly, no matter how much he loved the old one at Jackson's Mill.

One Sunday, before he went to Beverly to visit his sister, Tom invited a local girl, Miss Caroline Norris, to attend services with him at the Broad Run Church. The young West Point Cadet put on his dress uniform and saddled one of the finest horses at the mill for the excursion. The party of some half-dozen gathered at the Jackson home place and set off down river for the three-mile ride.

The road crossed the West Fork River several times and at Withers Ford near McCann's Run, the proud cadet suffered an intense embarrassment. While leading the way across the ford, Jackson's horse stumbled and went to its knees pitching the inattentive rider over its head and into three feet of water. As Tom picked himself up his face turned bright red at his discomfort. He stood there, dripping, while Miss Norris and the others asked about his condition and suggested that he return home for a change of clothes. With few words Jackson assured them he was fine and that his uniform would soon dry. He remounted and the party continued its journey. A number of biographers have attributed Jackson's insistence about continuing the trip to his politeness, stoicism or strict adherence to church doctrine. Obviously it was nothing quite so noble. While he stood in the river listening to the concerns of his friends, Tom most likely was thinking about the stories that would be told at his expense when the party arrived at the Broad Run Church. If anyone was going to relate the experience it would be he and besides, he had no intention of changing his clothes. He would not attend the service in his old homespuns; he would go in his uniform, no matter its condition.

This was a new Tom Jackson. Slowly but certainly he was coming out of his shell. During the last two years his education and experiences had greatly enhanced his confidence, knowledge, and self-image. Now he had friends at the Point and was becoming genuinely fond of debate with one or two of them. He was also beginning to discern the fact that there was more to life than grinding corn, sawing timber, or serving warrants. There was indeed another world out there and Tom Jackson, no matter the cost, intended to make a place in it for himself. That summer he told a cousin, "I am going to make a man of myself if I live."

Tom visited his sister Laura in Beverly that summer to meet her new husband, Jonathan Arnold, who was twenty-four years senior to his eighteen-year-old wife. It is safe to say that Tom's stay with them was not long as they were living in a boarding house at the time. Laura Jackson Arnold did not seem to want for much, although there was always some question as to just how happy the marriage was in those early years [See Appendix B for more on Laura Jackson].

Tom spent the rest of his leave at Jackson's Mill and in August, with less enthusiasm than he expected, Cadet Thomas Jonathan Jackson returned to West Point.

The author is featured on the back cover beside the unusual scroll headstone marking the gravesite of Laura Jackson Arnold. The grave is located in the Arnold plot near the top of a hill in the old section of the Heavner Cemetery in Buckhannon, West Virginia.

CHAPTER FIFTEEN

Things Change

Tom had spent part of his leave that summer helping his Uncle Cummins build a new house. The structure, on a rise across the road from the gristmill, was an ostentatious home of two stories built in the shape of an ell. The new Cummins Jackson home sported four fireplaces and lots of room. Tom felt good about the project and was now becoming more aware of just how much of an influential figure his uncle actually was.

The inscription on this marker states:

"This tablet marks the site of the boyhood home of

General T.J. (Stonewall) Jackson

A soldier of great military genius and renown

A man of resolute, pure and Christian character

DIED MAY 10, 1863

Of wounds received at the Battle of Chancellorsville, Virginia."

Once again, on the banks of the Hudson River, Tom found several changes had occurred during his leave. He had a new roommate and a new assignment. He was now an officer in the Corps of Cadets. Many biographers stated that Jackson was never a cadet officer but he documents the fact himself in a letter to his sister on September 8, 1884, "During my furlough I was made an officer, consequently my duties are lighter than usual."

Additionally, his course of study included such subjects as chemistry, mechanics, astronomy, optics and magnetism. Drawing was another subject that would give him difficulty. Tom threw himself into the academic regimen with fervor. By February his new roommate had resigned and alone in his room Tom would stoke the coal fire and study quietly into the early hours of the morning.

Not all of Jackson's reading was required reading. It was during this time he took an active interest in the life of Napoleon and acquired a fondness for the famous "maxims" of the emperor [See Appendix C for more maxims].

More and more, Tom Jackson was developing a rigid character born of long hours where his will and determination alone were the only way to success. Year by year the number of his demerits decreased as he became an almost perfect, if somewhat wooden, cadet. During the term prior to his leave, Tom became outraged when he found that someone had replaced his spotlessly clean musket with a dirty one. He reported the incident to a cadet officer and, since the Lewis County Cadet had secretly put a mark on his weapon, it was only the work of a few minutes to find the missing firearm in the rack of another cadet.

The furious Jackson demanded a Court of Honor and promised to testify against the miscreant. He would settle for nothing less than the thief's expulsion from the academy. Only insistent appeals from his fellow cadets convinced Jackson to change his mind. Thus, allowing a lesser punishment to be imposed.

With examinations approaching in May, Tom wrote to his sister that so far he had received no demerits for the academic year. His hope of improving his class ranking was also weighing heavily on his mind. He wrote, "If fortune should favor me in a degree corresponding to the past, I will have a better standing in my class than I have formerly had."

He was also becoming interested in politics and current events. In the same letter he asked Laura, "Let me know who is elected from Lewis County to the legislature, and also the Senator from the district, and the name and terms (cost of a subscription) of the democratic paper published in Clarksburg." Over the years at West Point his command of the English language was becoming impressive for a backwoods farm boy but his handwriting, especially his signature, was still atrocious.

When the results of the exams were published, Cadet Thomas J. Jackson had indeed advanced his standing. He was now twentieth in his class. In conduct he was number one.

With one year left at the Academy before graduation and feeling somewhat melancholy because he was not allowed leave to visit home, Jackson ruminated in a letter about his plans for the future. "I have before me two courses," he wrote, "either of which I may choose. The first would be to follow the profession of arms and the second, that of a civil pursuit, such as law. If I should adopt the first I could live independently and surrounded by friends who I have already made, and have no fear of want. My pay would be fixed; the principal thing I would have to attend to would be futurity."

"If I adopt the latter I presume that I would still find plenty of friends, but my exertions would have to be great in order to acquire a name. This course (the law) is most congenial to my taste, and consequently I expect to adopt it, after spending a few years in pursuing the former."

This passage is at once revealing. Nowhere is there a mention of the ministry, an often spoken desire of his early and late youth. Neither does there seem to be a great desire for a military career. There is also a distinct lapse of memory on Jackson's part concerning the document he signed (with blotted signature) at West Point on the twentieth day of February in 1843, when he swore to serve in the Army of the United States for eight years in exchange for his academy education. It is probable, however, that his case of homesickness generated these thoughts for he affirmed several times later that he had hopes of living near his sister, an objective that could only be attained through a civilian career.

As a cadet officer with more time for personal demands Jackson began to experience physical problems, or at least become more aware of them. As a result he spent much of his time on exercises which he believed might provide his restoration to perfect health. One physical exercise he took up was swinging a heavy broadsword. That, he felt, would strengthen his chest and have the desired effect. Jackson also went through similar exercises using a cavalry saber.

Academically he pursued excellence in his course on ethics, which he preferred to his other subjects of engineering, artillery, infantry tactics, mineralogy and geology. He felt that he might make the top five in his ethics course and admitted he was least interested in infantry tactics. He managed to place fifth in ethics, while his friend, George B. McClellan, was second.

By now Jackson's letters to his friends and family were sent at much longer intervals. His excuse, although he recognized it as a lame one, was the "strict requirements of many duties." It was, he told his sister, a partial if not complete justification.

It is possible the proximity of graduation was taking its toll. Later, on at least one occasion, Jackson admitted that feelings akin to homesickness for West Point had enveloped him the closer his graduation and ultimate departure came. There seems little doubt he had fallen for the academic life. His long hours of hard work had been productive and year by year, Thomas Jonathan Jackson was making his way toward the top of the list. At last he had become comfortable in a scholastic setting and he wasn't sure he wanted to leave it.

CHAPTER SIXTEEN

"Lieutenant Jackson"

The years at West Point had molded more than just the mind of Tom Jackson. Aware of the sobriquet "old Jackson" bestowed on him by fellow cadets, the Virginian did what he could to eradicate the reasons for it. Now, he no longer went about stoop-shouldered with head bowed. His posture was ramrod straight and at the dining table or study desk he sat rigidly erect. Added to his reading list were books on etiquette.

The new interest in politics and current events seemed to come at the right moment as rumors about a possible confrontation with Mexico circulated through the campus. [The United States declared war on Mexico in May 1846.]

Although dramatically changed from the slouching, awkward farm boy that entered West Point in 1842, Jackson still was considered by his instructors and classmates to possess a strong but not very quick mind. Tom admitted more than once that his memory was not very good, hence his practice of going over and over his lessons until he felt sure he could retain their content.

The final exams before graduation were evidence that Tom's drive and determination were gaining the goals he had set for himself. He ranked eleventh in mineralogy and geology, twelfth in engineering, eleventh in artillery, twenty-first in infantry tactics and fifth in ethics. He had received only seven demerits for the year and in his final standing was ranked seventh in his class. Later, several of his fellow cadets said if there had been just one more year before graduation Thomas Jackson would have ranked number one.

That honor, however, went to Charles S. Stewart of New Jersey who never attained General Officer rank. Number two in Jackson's class was George B. McClellan

One of the upper classmen, when Jackson came to West Point, had noted that he was "like unto a cake unturned." A biblical way, he said, of saying that young Thomas Jackson was a diamond in the rough.

Upon graduation Thomas Jonathan Jackson was commissioned a Second Lieutenant in the United States Army and assigned to Artillery. Although the war with Mexico had already started, Tom was granted a short leave. He immediately packed his belongings and set out for Jackson's Mill. He had not had a letter from his Uncle Cummins or any other member of his family in Lewis County for two years. Nor had he written to any of them during that time.

Jackson and four other new second lieutenants left West Point in early July. They stopped overnight at the

Brown Hotel in Washington where they all consumed more than their fair share of food and drink. When Tom got on the train the next morning he was suffering from the first real hangover of his life. He decided he did indeed like the taste of hard liquor but he wasn't very fond of the after-effects. He seldom touched the stuff thereafter.

He arrived in Weston on July 20, 1846, after a short visit with his sister in Beverly. It was a Monday and the town was full of activity. The local militia had been called out and the unit members were on every street corner trying to recruit enough men to form a volunteer company for the war.

Tom, wearing a sparkling new officer's uniform, was quickly spotted by the local militia commander, a Colonel McKinley. He insisted that the young officer take command for some parade ground drill, probably with the hope that a decent show might induce more of the local men to sign up for the volunteer company. As it turned out Jackson could not hear and misinterpreted the Colonel's orders and the company headed off in a direction different than the militia commander had intended.

Before he left the group of aspiring soldiers Tom informed them that he expected orders at any moment.

"I want to see you at the taking of the city of Mexico" he told his fellow Lewis Countians. "We are going to take it!" he declared.

Jackson spent that evening and all day Tuesday in a joyful reunion with his relatives and friends at Jackson's Mill and, for the first time, slept in the new house he had helped his Uncle Cummins build. Doubtlessly he spent some time in his favorite places: sitting against the sycamore tree at the end of the dam and escaping the late July sun under the shade of his beloved maple trees in the south meadow.

As he suspected, his idle time was to be short. On Wednesday, July 22, he received orders to report to a Captain Francis Taylor at Fort Columbus on Governor's Island in

New York. Tom Jackson left his home at Jackson's Mill on the following day beginning a journey that would propel him into military history. He would rest under the shade of his trees again several times, but only briefly.[11]

It had been almost four years to the day when the young man from the mountains of Western Virginia had opened a new notebook and written,

"You may be whatever you resolve to be."

Endnotes

[1] The son, William Wirt Woodson, was born on October 7, 1831. He was raised by his mother's brother Alfred Neal in Parkersburg, West Virginia.

[2] Jonathan Jackson was the third son of Edward and Mary Hadden Jackson. Mary Hadden died in 1796 and Edward married Elizabeth Brake three years later. The first son of that union was Cummins Jackson.

[3] The West Fork of the Monogahela River was larger in those days with significantly more volume. In 1934 the channel was straightened to its present course.

[4] The quote comes from a letter written to his sister Laura on September 8, 1844 while Jackson was a cadet at West Point.

[5] Mary (Polly) Hadden Jackson, Jonathan's sister, married Isaac Brake in November of 1820.

[6] It is possible the mill was under construction as early as 1838. The family, however, did not arrive in Lewis County until 1840.

[7] Thaddeus Moore died in Clarksburg, Virginia before the beginning of the Civil War.

[8] The use of the middle initial in the two petitions and Tom Jackson's letter of acceptance written on June 18, 1842, show that statements by some biographers, which attribute the adoption of the middle initial to the fact that his mail was being mixed up with another Cadet Jackson at West Point, are in error. It is true, however, that there was a problem with his mail at the academy, especially concerning letters from his sister, Laura, who continued to address him as Cadet Thomas Jackson.

Jackson mentioned the issue in a letter to his sister on February 10, 1845. He wrote, "You will please direct your subsequent letters to Thos. J. Jackson, for there is some difficulty in obtaining them from the post office on account of another cadet's name being Thos. K. Jackson."

[9] Author Edward C. Smith, in his sketch of Jackson, states that Congressman Hayes wrote to the Superintendent of the Military Academy requesting that the examination be made easy for Jackson. While possible, it is highly unlikely that Hayes, after the embarrassment caused by Gibson Butcher, would attempt to influence the procedure beyond his letter of recommendation to the Secretary of War. At any rate there is no evidence existent that Hayes requested or Jackson received any help with the exams.

[10] The south barracks were demolished in 1849 and the north barracks were torn down two years later in 1851.

[11] He would not return to Jackson's Mill until December 1848. His last visit would take place in 1857.

APPENDIX A- *Joseph Lightburn*

Joseph Lightburn enlisted in the army at Newport Barracks, Kentucky, in 1846 to fight in the war with Mexico. He spent the next five years at various army posts in the United States and was discharged as a sergeant in 1851 without seeing combat. He returned to Lewis County and worked as a farmer and miller and became a preacher of the Baptist faith in 1859. In 1861 Joe Lightburn was one of the five delegates to the Wheeling Convention that was called to discuss the formation of the new state of West Virginia. By August he had been commissioned a colonel and given command of the Fourth West Virginia Infantry Regiment and soon was named Commander of the Kanawha District where he was successfully tested in the fighting around that valley.

By 1862 Lightburn had moved his regiment to Vicksburg where, at the direction of General Ulysses S.

Grant, it participated in the effort to cut a canal and isolate the strongly fortified city.

While on his way home for a well-deserved leave Colonel Lightburn was stopping over in Wheeling when the Jones-Imboden raid sent shock waves through what is now central West Virginia. The raid went through the central part of the state and through Lighburn's hometown of Weston. As the ranking officer in the area he was given immediate command of the region until he returned to his regular duties in May.

Back in Vicksburg his regiment participated in a charge of the Confederate fortifications and suffered numerous casualties. Twenty-five men of the Fourth West Virginia Infantry were killed that day and ten others soon died from wounds received in the assault. Lightburn escaped injury when one bullet hit his sword and another passed through his coat.

By March 1863, Joseph Andrew Jackson Lightburn was commissioned a brigadier general and fought in the battle of Chattanooga, before joining Sherman's march to the sea. On August 24, 1864, General Joseph Lightburn was shot in the forehead by a Confederate marksman and knocked from his horse. He went home to Broad Run to recuperate and was then reassigned to the Department of West Virginia and stationed in Harpers Ferry. It was during this assignment he met a young captain named William McKinley. At the time, neither man had any reason to suspect the brilliant but short future destiny had decreed for one of them. This was, of course, William McKinnley destined to become the 25th President of the United States, and the second President to be assassinated.

In January, 1865, General Lightburn was given command of the First Brigade of the Second Infantry Division. He was ordered to guard the Baltimore & Ohio Railroad lines from Parkersburg to Cumberland, Maryland.

Two months after the war ended Lightburn submitted his resignation and returned home where he was the guest of honor, during the Independence Day celebrations in Weston, and the recipient of an engraved sword presented by the citizens of Lewis County. Joe Lightburn continued to minister and in 1866 became a member of the State Legislature. After nearly ten years pastoring churches in Pennsylvania and southern West Virginia, he returned to his home in Lewis County and became the pastor of the Broad Run Church.

In May of 1901 Joseph Andrew Jackson Lightburn fell ill with pneumonia and died at the age of seventy-seven. *It had been thirty-eight years since his boyhood friend Tom Jackson had also succumbed to the same illness that was a complication from his battle wounds, in the same month, far away from the homeplace at Jackson's Mill and his down-river friend.*

APPENDIX B- *Laura Jackson Arnold*

Whatever the quality of the union between Laura Jackson Arnold and Jonathan Arnold, it produced four children. The last one, a daughter, died not long after her birth in December of 1853.

From all accounts, Laura's religious feelings did not run as deep as her brother's and Tom often expressed his concern about this to other members of the family. During the war, Beverly, for the most part, was occupied by union troops and beginning with the battle of Rich Mountain in July of 1861, the Arnold House, on the corner of Main Street, became a hospital,

Laura went to work as a volunteer nurse, tending wounded from both sides. She was, however, pro-union and at one point sent a letter to President Lincoln supporting his efforts to hold the country together. At some juncture her husband began to get jealous of Laura's mothering ways with the soldiers and trouble developed in the marriage.

Jonathan Arnold was arrested for disloyalty, a charge so vague that the commanding general, stationed in Clarksburg, paroled him. Arnold seriously felt that Laura had somehow caused his arrest and after the war sued her for divorce. He charged his young wife with giving some soldiers more than the loving care of a nurse or mother. One witness even testified he had seen Laura Jackson in bed with a union officer. The court decided in Jonathan Arnold's favor and Laura had to pay the court costs. She did, however, get four hundred dollars a year in alimony.

After the divorce Laura went to Buckhannon where she lived, off and on, until her death on September 24, 1911. In a letter to her sister-in-law in 1903 Laura Arnold made a statement that nearly echoed her brother's dying words,". . . My nearest relatives have nearly all passed over the river." She was buried in Heavner Cemetery just north of Buckhannon.

APPENDIX C- *Jackson's Maxims*

Although Tom Jackson began his book of

"Maxims" upon his entry into West Point, it was some eight

months before he borrowed Scott's "Napoleon" from the

academy library. It has been said that he so enjoyed

Napoleon's list of maxims that he almost always had a copy

of them within reach. It is not hard to see how his private

notebook became a place where he listed his own

"maxims." What follows, then, is a list of sayings Jackson

strived to adhere to, during the rest of his life.

Jackson's Maxims

You may be what ever you resolve to be.

Sacrifice your life rather than your word.

Disregard public opinion when it interferes with your duty.

Endeavor to do well, everything you undertake.

Endeavor to be at peace with all men.

Lose no time; be always employed in something useful; cut off unnecessary actions.

Speak but what may benefit others or yourself. Avoid trifling conversation.

Be not disturbed at trifles, nor accidents, common or unavoidable.

It is not desirable to have a large number of intimate friends.

Be kind, condescending and affable.

Resolve to perform what you ought; perform without fail what you resolve.

There is danger in catching the habits of your associates.

Through life let your principal object be the discharge of duty.

Never speak disrespectfully of anyone without a cause.

David:

Thought you might enjoy these!

— Gordon

Teachers change the world!

Waste nothing.

Eat not to dullness, drink not to elevation.

Never weary your company by talking too long or too frequently.

Never try to appear more wise or learned than the rest of the company.

The means by which men are to attain great elevation may be classed in three divisions: physical, mental and moral.

Seek those who are intelligent and virtuous.

Always look people in the face when addressing them, and generally when they address you.

Bibliography

Adams, Julia Davis. *Stonewall*. New York, New York, 1931.

Arnold, Thomas Jackson. *The Early Life and Letters of General Thomas J. Jackson*. New York, New York 1916.

Baxter, Phyllis. *Laura Jackson Arnold*. A term paper. West Virginia University. Morgantown, West Virginia.

Chase, William C. *Story of Stonewall Jackson*. Atlanta, Georgia, 1901. (This biography was approved by Jackson's widow Mary Anna Jackson).

Cook, Roy Bird. *The Family and Early Life of Stonewall Jackson*. Richmond, Virginia, 1924.

Meador, Michael M. *Historic Jackson's Mill, A Walking Tour*. Parsons, West Virginia, 1991.

Roy Bird Cook Collection. West Virginia University Library. Morgantown, West Virginia.

Smith, Edward C. *Thomas Jonathan Jackson, A Sketch*. Weston, West Virginia, 1920.

State Archives. West Virginia Cultural Center. Charleston, West Virginia.

West Virginia Archeologist. Vol. 37 (1) Spring, 1985.

West Virginia University Dorsey Resource Center, Jackson's Mill. Weston, West Virginia.